MYSTERIES OF MIGRATION

A caribou herd migrates to summer grazing grounds in Alaska.

MYSTERIES OF MIGRATION

By Robert M. McClung

GARRARD PUBLISHING COMPANY
CHAMPAIGN, ILLINOIS

Photo Credits

Ron Austing from NAS Collection/Photo Researchers: pp. 10
Ron Austing from Photo Researchers: pp. 57
A. Avis from Bruce Coleman Inc.: pp. 6
Jen and Des Bartlett from Bruce Coleman Inc.: pp. 60
Mark Boulton from Photo Researchers: pp. 35
Jane Burton from Bruce Coleman Inc.: pp. 46 (top)
George W. Calef from Photo Researchers: pp. 26
Jim Cartier from Photo Researchers: pp. 53
Richard H. Chesher from Photo Researchers: pp. 34
Stephen Dalton from Photo Researchers: pp. 46 (bottom)
Jeff Foott from Bruce Coleman Inc.: pp. 27, 37, 43
Kenneth M. Highfill from Photo Researchers: pp. 51
Karl W. Kenyon from NAS Collection/Photo Researchers: pp. 30
Stephen J. Krasemann from Photo Researchers: pp. 14
James C. Leupold from U.S. Fish and Wildlife Service: pp. 12
Stephen Maslowski from Photo Researchers: pp. 15
National Audubon Society/Photo Researchers: pp. 55
Charlie Ott from NAS Collection/Photo Researchers: pp. 2
Len Rue Jr. from Photo Researchers: pp. 24
Leonard Lee Rue III from Freelance Photographers: pp. 50 (both)
Leonard Lee Rue III from NAS Collection/Photo Researchers: pp. 38
Leonard Lee Rue III from Photo Researchers: pp. 62
David C. Rentz from Bruce Coleman Inc.: pp. 49
Alfred Renfro from Photo Researchers: pp. 59
Laura Riley from Bruce Coleman Inc: pp. 1
Frank Schleicher from Photo Researchers: pp. 17
Marilyn Stouffer from Photo Researchers: pp. 19
U.S. Fish & Wildlife Service: pp. 5
Ron Winch From Photo Researchers: pp. 18
Jeanne White from Photo Researchers: pp. 22

Cover Photograph by David Hefferman from U.S. Fish & Wildlife Service

Spot Art and Maps by Benjamin C. Blake

Library of Congress Cataloging in Publication Data

McClung, Robert M.
   Mysteries of migration.

   Includes index.
   Summary: Discusses why some animals, including the
Arctic tern, northern fur seal, and Pacific salmon,
migrate, while others do not, where the migrants go,
how they get there, and how long they stay.
      1. Animal migration—Juvenile literature. [1. Animals
—Migration] I. Title.
QL754.M36 1982   591.52′5   82-15740
ISBN 0-8116-2950-3

Contents

Snow geese often fly in V-formation as they travel between southern wintering grounds and nesting areas in the Arctic.

1. By Land, by Sea, and in the Air

Spring is the time when many animals are making long journeys from their winter to their summer homes. Many bird travelers are seen in the northern United States at this time. Red-winged blackbirds sway on dried reeds in the marshes and call to one another. Okalee! Okalee! They have just arrived from South America. Robins look for worms on our lawns, and geese fly in V-formations overhead. All have wintered further south.

Soon the loud whistle of the northern oriole is heard. It is back from its winter home in Central America. Bobolinks and swallows appear after a long journey from South America.

Spring is also the time when frogs and toads chorus in our ponds. After their long winter sleep, male frogs and toads travel to the ponds first. They croak and trill, calling for females to come to the ponds too.

In the spring deer and elk that wintered in sheltered western valleys begin to move up into the hills and mountains where they will spend the summer. Spring is the time when shad and alewives, a kind of herring, leave the sea and begin to swim upstream. They will mate and lay their eggs in fresh water. Whales begin to travel northward to summer feeding grounds in Arctic waters. Fur seals start the long journey back to their remote breeding grounds in the Bering Sea, west of Alaska.

In autumn animals leave their summer breeding and feeding grounds and head for winter homes. These regular seasonal journeys from one area to another are called migrations. Most animals that migrate make the round trip between two homes every year. But others that migrate like the Pacific salmon and the eel make the round trip just once in a lifetime.

Why Animals Migrate

Most animals that migrate would die or have a very hard time finding food and shelter if they stayed in one area the year round.

Many birds leave their summer nesting areas each fall because they cannot find enough food there during the cold winter. They travel to a warmer climate where food is plentiful and shelter is adequate. But when springtime comes, they return to their summer nesting areas.

Food, shelter, and suitable breeding grounds are the main reasons why animals migrate. Just as birds migrate because of these needs, so do whales and fur seals, elk and caribou, and many other animals.

Changes in weather conditions trigger migration for many animals. Seasonal changes in the number of hours of daylight and in the temperature of the air or water may start the migrants on their journeys.

The increase or decrease in the number of daylight hours affects the production of hormones by various glands in a bird's body. These hormones affect the bird's general behavior as well as its readiness for courtship and nesting. In springtime the bird is stimulated to start the journey to its breeding grounds; in the fall it journeys to its winter home.

Before birds start to migrate in the fall, they store up large amounts of fat in their bodies. They will use the fat as fuel to nourish them and give them energy on the long flight to their winter homes.

2. *Birds,*
Feathered Followers of the Sun

Of all animals, birds are the best known for their long journeys each spring and fall. About two-thirds of the 660 species of birds that spend part of every year in the United States migrate between summer and winter homes. Billions of birds travel the flyways over North America every spring and fall.

Some birds fly only a few hundred miles, or less, between summer and winter homes. Many robins, crows, and bluejays are in this group. Other species may migrate thousands of miles each year.

A few birds, such as hummingbirds and falcons, usually travel by themselves. Others migrate in huge flocks that can number in the thousands. Waterfowl often fly in lines or V-formations. Some birds seldom fly higher than the treetops; others may travel at altitudes of many thousands of feet. They may have to fly high to cross mountains or to take advantage of wind currents.

Some species migrate by day; others fly during the night. Those that fly at night stop to feed and rest during the daylight hours. Some make almost incredible nonstop flights.

The ruby-throated hummingbird is the smallest bird found in eastern North America. It weighs just a tenth of an ounce. When migration time comes, about one-third of the hummingbird's weight is fat. The fat provides fuel for the bird's nonstop flight across the Gulf of Mexico to Mexico and Central America. The overnight trip takes about 25 hours. During every second of the time, each of the hummingbird's wings beats about 50 times—3,000 times every minute!

Many warblers and other small land birds fly nonstop over the Atlantic Ocean and the Caribbean Sea to South America. They accomplish this over-water passage of 2,300 miles in about 86 hours. Scientists who track these migrants by radar, both on ships and on shore, report that these little land birds sometimes fly at altitudes of 21,000 feet to take advantage of favorable winds.

Arctic Tern

The prize for long-distance commuting every year probably goes to the Arctic tern. This fork-tailed seabird has a black cap and a bloodred beak. It nests on the Arctic tundra around the North Pole where the sun never sets during the summer. The birds enjoy 24 hours of daylight in which to hunt for food for their hungry young.

By the time the young birds are able to fly, the short Arctic summer is almost over. Then the terns begin the long journey to their winter home. Leaving the tundra, they fly southward over the North

Atlantic Ocean, close to the coasts of Europe and Africa. They follow ocean currents that swarm with little fish and shrimp that are their main food. Onward they fly over the South Atlantic, until they reach the shores of Patagonia and Antarctica.

It is summer in the southern hemisphere when the terns are there. Once again they enjoy almost 24 hours of daylight every day. Before the Antarctic winter sets in, the terns start the long trip back toward the North Pole. When they arrive, it will be springtime and nesting time in the Arctic. These terns travel 11,000 miles each way, a 22,000-mile round trip each year.

Golden Plover

Some birds follow one route on their fall migration and a different one on the return trip next spring. The American golden plover is one of these. It is a handsome shorebird with black underparts, a gold-flecked back, and a broad white band across its forehead and neck.

After raising its young on the Arctic tundra, as the Arctic terns do, American golden plovers travel southeastward when it is time for fall migration. Passing over Labrador and Nova Scotia, they head southward over the Atlantic Ocean and fly nonstop over the water to South America. They spend the winter (summer in the southern hemisphere) in Argentina. There they feed on insects and berries.

When the time comes for their return trip to the Arctic, the plovers follow an inland route. They head northward over the jungles of Brazil, Central America, and Mexico; then they fly on across the prairies of the United States and Canada. Along the way they stop frequently to feed. Finally they reach their nesting grounds in the Arctic.

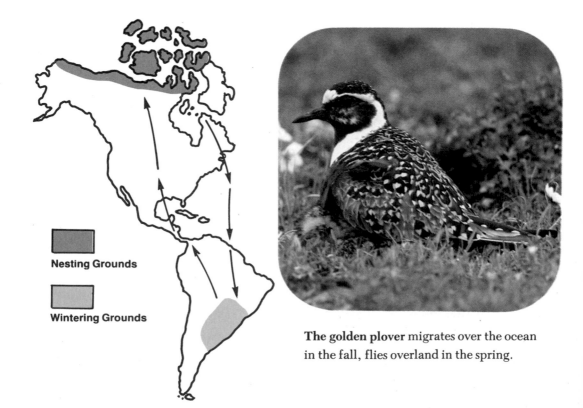

Nesting Grounds

Wintering Grounds

The golden plover migrates over the ocean in the fall, flies overland in the spring.

The chimney swift nests and roosts inside chimneys throughout the United States. For many years its winter home was unknown.

Chimney Swift

Scientists learn what routes migrating birds fly and where they go by putting identifying rings or bands on the legs of individual birds. Later they may get a report that one of these banded birds is picked up in another area. They then know that the bird flew there from the spot where it was banded. That is how the mystery of the chimney swift's winter home was finally solved.

A sooty-colored little bird with long narrow wings and tiny feet, the chimney swift is a common summer resident throughout the United States and southern Canada. It zigs and zags in batlike flight over towns and cities and eats insects while in flight. Using their saliva as glue, swifts fasten their flimsy twig nests to the inside walls of chimneys or hollow trees. They roost in these enclosed places, sometimes in great numbers. As many as 7,000 of them have been seen descending into one chimney. Banders can easily capture swifts in such roosts and band them all.

In the fall, chimney swifts leave these nesting and roosting places and disappear. For centuries the location of their winter home remained unknown. In the effort to trace their travels, more than half a million chimney swifts were banded in the early years of this century. None of those bands was recovered from the wintering area until 1944.

That year South American Indians living in the jungles near the headwaters of the Amazon River brought thirteen small bird bands to a missionary who had befriended them. The bands had been taken from birds gathered in the remote Yanayaco Valley, east of Lima, Peru. When the numbers on those bands were checked, scientists discovered that the chimney swifts had been banded in several different areas of the United States. The winter home of the swifts was discovered at last.

A red-tailed hawk soars aloft on drafts of warm air.

3. How Birds Find Their Way

Migrations of birds have been observed and studied more than those of any other group. The more we learn about bird migrations, the more remarkable they seem.

How do birds know in what direction to fly above thousands of miles of open ocean from their summer homes to their winter ones? How are they able to find their way back to their summer homes, sometimes to the very same tree or yard in which they nested the year before?

Visual Landmarks

We often go from one place to another by following visual landmarks that we know and recognize. A hike from home to a favorite picnic spot may take us past the school and public library and then on to

the outskirts of town. We may then climb a steep
hill and head for the woodland beyond. Perhaps a
big oak tree marks the spot where we enter the
woods. Then we may follow a narrow woodland path
until we reach a brook. We may then follow the
brook until it becomes a pond. Halfway around the
pond is a big boulder which is a favorite picnic spot.

Migrating birds and other animals take advantage
of landmarks they see in much the same way. Some
birds follow the coastline. Others follow rivers,

◀ **Canada geese**, flying in close formation, follow rivers and other natural landmarks in their migrations.

which are natural trails that lead to the sea. Other landmarks may be lakes or mountain ranges or individual mountain peaks.

The Appalachian Mountain range stretches from southern New York to Alabama. It is a natural pathway that many hawks and eagles follow in their north-south journeys. Scarcely moving their wings, these birds of prey ride the thermals–drafts of warm air that rise between the ridges. If conditions are just right at Hawk Mountain in Pennsylvania, observers sometimes count 5,000 or more migrating hawks on a fall day.

Waterfowl and shorebirds fly age-old routes called "flyways" during migration. One flyway follows the Atlantic coastline of North America, another the Pacific Coast, a third goes through the center of the continent following the Mississippi River valley, and a fourth goes through the Great Plains. All these flyways have distinctive features which birds can see and follow.

In many parts of the world, prevailing winds blow in a particular direction at certain seasons of the year. Birds may take advantage of these winds in their travels.

The Sun and Stars

For centuries sailors have used visual landmarks to help chart their ship's course at sea. They also take advantage of prevailing winds and currents. In addition, they use a navigational instrument called a sextant to measure the altitude of heavenly bodies–the sun, moon, planets, and stars–above the horizon at any given time. This shows them their north-south position, or latitude. They use another instrument called a chronometer as a time clock. With this they can determine their east-west position, or longitude.

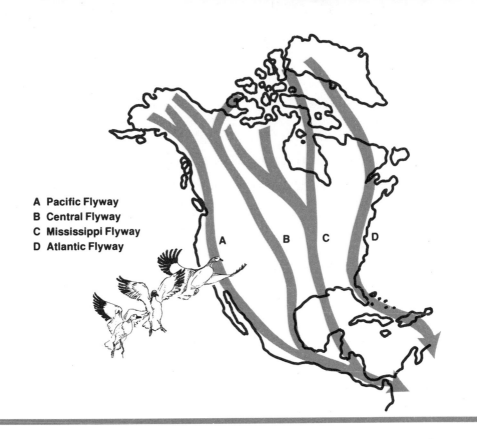

A Pacific Flyway
B Central Flyway
C Mississippi Flyway
D Atlantic Flyway

There are four main aerial highways
for migrating birds in North America.

Birds and other animal migrants can chart their way, as sailors do, by observing the positions of the stars or sun. However, their instruments are built into their bodies. Experiments show that night-flying birds determine the direction they want to go by observing star patterns in the sky above them. Day fliers use the sun as a guide. Their biological or built-in time clocks enable birds to chart their directions from the stars or sun even though the positions of these bodies change constantly.

Built-in Compass

Sailors have compasses in their ships to point the way to true North. Recent experiments with pigeons, honeybees, and bacteria show that these creatures have magnetic substances within their body tissues that act as built-in compasses. Thus the animals are able to position themselves in relation to the earth's magnetic field, which indicates the direction of true North.

This may help to explain the remarkable homing ability of pigeons and other birds. Pigeons can be taken from their familiar roosts to some distant point where they have never been before. When they are released, the pigeons fly upward and circle until they get their bearings. Then they head back in the direction of their home roost.

Dangers Along the Way

In spite of their ability to find their way from summer to winter homes and back, birds face many hazards along the way. They usually begin their journeys when the weather is favorable, but the weather can change. The migrating birds may fly into snow or freezing rain in an area where they cannot find food or shelter.

Lighthouses, radio beacons, and skyscrapers also pose dangers. Flocks of birds flying at night are often confused by powerful searchlight beams, especially when it is cloudy or foggy. They may fly directly into the light or crash into the tall building or beacon.

In spite of such accidents, the real marvel of migration is that so many birds are able to complete their journeys successfully. These master navigators are able to chart their paths through the skies from their summer to winter homes and back.

4. Mammal Journeys

Many mammals undertake long journeys each year. Bats are the only mammals that can fly. They migrate through the air as birds do. Hoary and red bats fly hundreds of miles southward each fall to spend the winter in warmer areas. Some bats fly to caves where they hibernate during the winter. They show remarkable homing ability by going back to the same caves year after year.

Some grazing animals make spectacular overland migrations. In East Africa, gazelles, wildebeests, and other hoofed mammals graze in the open woodlands during the dry season. When the rainy season starts, vast herds migrate to the plains of the Serengeti, now green with newly sprouted grass and other vegetation. In North America, caribou make similar journeys between summer grazing areas and more sheltered winter areas.

Hoofed Animals in North America

In the caribou country of northern Canada and Alaska, springtime comes quickly. As heavy snows and the ice on rivers melt, loud cracks and booms can be heard as ice floes start to move. A tinge of green comes to the treeless tundra. This is the time when caribou, the American reindeer, begin their long journey from their winter homes along the edge of the northern forests to summer grazing areas in the tundra.

The cows start the long journey first. Small bands gather into huge herds, and soon countless thousands of caribou are plodding northward. The caribou follow age-old trails that are rutted and marked by the marches of countless generations. Their wide-spreading hooves seem to click, but the sound is made by the movement of ankle bones or tendons.

When they reach an ice-laden river, the cows

plunge in and swim across. Sometimes many drown in the swift and icy waters. Indians and Eskimos wait at certain spots to kill the caribou cows for their meat and hides. Wolves follow the vast herds and pick off stragglers, weakened old animals, and calves which are born along the way.

A herd of caribou splash across a river as they make their way to summer feeding grounds.

Bison once roamed the western plains by the millions. Today this herd lives in Custer State Park, South Dakota.

Bull caribou follow the cows a couple of weeks later. All summer long the herds graze on lichens and grasses on the tundra. When fall comes, they begin the long trek back to their winter quarters.

Over a century ago American buffalo, or bison, roamed the western prairies in countless millions. Many of them made similar long journeys from southern wintering grounds to summer grazing areas and back each year. Sometimes they traveled in vast herds. In 1871 a troop of U.S. cavalrymen watched such a herd as it passed through the valley of the Arkansas River. The herd covered an area about 25 miles in width and 50 miles in length, and it took several days for all the buffalo to pass. The soldiers calculated that the herd contained about four million buffalo.

In western mountain areas elk and deer make shorter and less spectacular migrations every year between summer grazing grounds in high mountain meadows and sheltered lowland valleys where they spend the winter. The National Elk Refuge in Jackson, Wyoming, just south of Yellowstone National Park, is the scene of the largest winter gathering of elk in North America. Before the area was settled, the elk found plenty of winter food in the valley. Today ranch fences keep the animals away from most of their old grazing grounds. So the refuge staff scatters hay every day throughout the winter for 7,000 or more elk. Without this goverment handout the animals would starve.

Northern Fur Seal

Many mammals of the sea travel thousands of miles through the oceans each year as they migrate between breeding and feeding grounds. The northern fur seal is one of the best known of these travelers.

The principal breeding grounds of this species are the Pribilof Islands, which are small dots in the Bering Sea. The big burly bulls haul themselves out on the rocky coasts in May. They fight among themselves for beach rights and stake out breeding territories. The female seals arrive in June. Wherever a female comes ashore, it is immediately claimed by the resident bull. Young males also arrive at this time. Unable to compete with the older bulls for mates, the young males take up residence on "bachelor" beaches. Over a million seals gather on these small islands every summer.

The pregnant females give birth to pups within a few days of their arrival. Several days later they mate with the resident bull. All summer they nurse their young and look after them. The females go to sea for several days at a time to hunt for food. When they return, each mother seal is able to locate her pup among thousands of babies. Its distinctive voice and smell guide her to it.

By October the young seals are weaned. Then the mother seals leave their young and swim out to sea for their long winter journey to warmer waters.

Some of them swim as far south as the coastal waters off California and Mexico.

When their mothers do not return, the pups soon leave the Pribilof Islands. They swim through the waters of the Pacific for many months. Seldom, if ever, do they go ashore until they head back to the Pribilofs as two-year-old females or bachelors.

The big bulls are usually the last of the fur seals

to leave the islands every fall. They generally remain in the Bering Sea during the winter and are the first seals back at the breeding grounds in the spring.

Whales Feed in Polar Regions

While the fur seals are breeding in the Pribilof Islands each summer, gray whales are feeding in the food-rich Arctic seas and putting on thick coats of blubber. As fall approaches, the whales leave these far northern feeding grounds and start a long 5,000-mile journey to their winter home and breeding grounds. Traveling at about five miles an hour and as much as a hundred miles a day, the gray whales head southward. During the long journey they evidently feed very little and live mainly off their fat.

They pass just a few miles off the California coast. Whale watchers often observe them from boats or viewing towers. By December the whales reach the warm waters off Baja California. There they will spend the winter.

Great numbers of them gather in Scammon Lagoon, which the Mexican government set aside as a whale refuge in 1972. Pregnant females give birth to their calves in these warm, protected waters, and bulls court unmated cows. In early springtime most of the whales leave the area and start the long trip back to their northern feeding grounds.

All the big whales make similar journeys every year as they travel from feeding grounds in polar areas to warmer waters closer to the equator. In

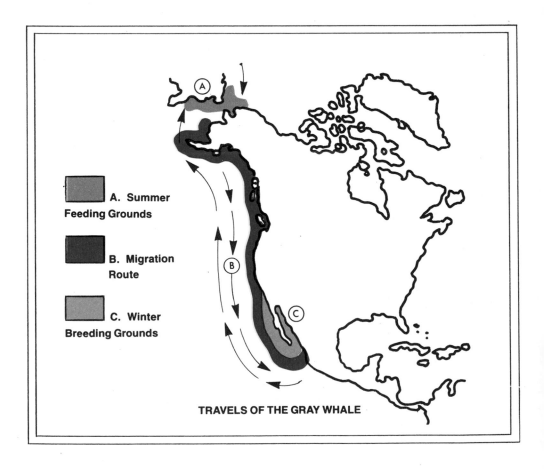

A. Summer Feeding Grounds

B. Migration Route

C. Winter Breeding Grounds

TRAVELS OF THE GRAY WHALE

their travels they often follow the coastlines of different continents. Perhaps they are guided in their journeys by distinctive features of the ocean floor. They may recognize ocean currents and follow them as well. Some observers believe that whales may also use the sun and stars to help them chart their courses.

Whales are famous for the songs they sometimes sing underwater. The songs are a strange mixture of groans, chirps, trills, and rising or falling notes. Some scientists believe that these noises may be used by whales to communicate with one another. The blue whale's voice, it is said, can be heard by other whales through hundreds of miles of salt water.

Gray whales breed in the waters off Baja California. Mexico made Scammon Lagoon a refuge for the species in 1972.

5. *Fish, Frogs,*
and Other Cold-Blooded Travelers

Very few amphibians or reptiles make long migratory journeys. Many, however, do make short trips every year from winter shelters to breeding areas. In springtime frogs and toads leave the places where they hibernate and make their way to the ponds where they will mate and lay their eggs. Awakened by the first spring rains, spotted salamanders crawl out of their winter shelters in the woods and also head for breeding ponds.

Every fall, snakes in cold regions travel to sheltered places where they will hibernate during the winter. Garter snakes and rattlesnakes may travel several miles every year to return to the same winter dens. The only snakes known to make long journeys are sea snakes. They sometimes gather in great numbers in certain ocean areas where they mate.

Sea Turtles

The giant sea turtles are reptiles that make long journeys. They sometimes travel thousands of miles

After digging a nest hole with her hind legs, **the green turtle** lays her eggs and then covers them with sand.

from ocean feeding grounds to beaches where the females come ashore to lay their eggs. Investigators who have tagged green turtles have found that many of them feed off the coasts of Brazil and travel 1,500 miles or more to tiny Ascension Island in the South Atlantic to lay their eggs. Once the eggs are laid, they return to the coastal waters off Brazil.

How do the turtles find their way to and from this little island in the middle of the ocean? Perhaps the temperature and chemistry of the ocean currents help to guide them. Perhaps they have the ability to navigate by using the sun and stars.

Many saltwater fish migrate thousands of miles through the seas every year as they move from feeding to breeding grounds. Tuna are great travelers. So are the herring and the anchovies that tuna feed upon.

A few fish make long journeys between salt and fresh water for feeding and breeding. Among these are the salmon and the eel.

Pacific Salmon

When springtime comes to the the swift-flowing streams of western North America, tiny salmon

Each baby salmon, or alevin, has a yolk sac when it first hatches. The yolk sac nourishes it for several weeks.

break out of round pea-sized eggs hidden among the pebbles in the stream bottom. Less than half an inch long when they hatch, the little salmon live in the stream until they are about two years old and six to eight inches in length. Then they begin long journeys downstream to the larger parent river and finally to the sea.

For four years or more the salmon grow as they feed in the ocean. During that time they may swim 1,500 miles or more away from the mouth of their home river. Eventually, as full grown adults, they make the journey back to fresh water to spawn and lay their eggs.

No one knows just how the salmon find their way from the ocean back to their original streams, but they do get there. Perhaps they remember the ocean currents and changing temperatures of the waters they swam through years before. The distinctive smell and chemical composition of the waters of the parent river help to guide them.

Making their way into the mouth of the home river, the salmon swim upstream. Along the way they face many dangers. They have to leap over falls and swim past rapids. As they struggle through foaming white waters, they are often dashed against rocks and injured. Big brown bears, eagles, and other fish-eating animals feast on the salmon as they travel upstream. Sometimes the waters they swim through are polluted by factory wastes or insecticides. Then many salmon may die.

The survivors continue upstream, "sampling" or smelling the waters of every tributary they reach. At last they approach the mouth of the stream where they hatched. They recognize its distinctive smell and turn into the stream. This is where they will mate and lay their eggs. Then they too will die.

Long Journeys of Eels

The eel's travels are just the opposite. Female eels live their adult lives in freshwater ponds or streams that empty into the Atlantic Ocean. The males live in brackish bays and inlets closer to the sea. When they are eight to fifteen years old and ready to mate, the female American eels leave their freshwater homes and travel down to salt water. Then they swim a thousand miles or more southeastward through the Atlantic Ocean. Male eels make the same journey. Finally the eels arrive at the Sargasso Sea, southeast of Bermuda.

There, at a depth of 1,000 feet or more, the female eels lay their tiny eggs and the males fertilize them. After that the adult eels die.

The eggs hatch into tiny larval eels called leptocephali. Leaflike and transparent, the quarter-inch-long larvae do not look like adult eels. Soon they

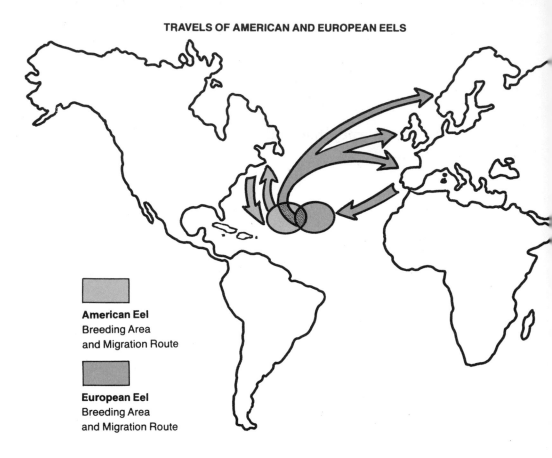

American Eel
Breeding Area
and Migration Route

European Eel
Breeding Area
and Migration Route

start the long year-and-a-half journey to the coast of
North America. Ocean currents help them along.

As they approach the coast, the leptocephali
transform into little three-inch-long eels. At this
stage they are known as elvers. The male elvers stay
in the inlets, but the females head upstream in fresh
water. Sometimes they travel hundreds of miles to
an inland lake. They may stay there to grow up.

European eels also lay their eggs in the Sargasso

Sea. The journey back to Europe takes their young nearly three years.

For many centuries no one knew where eels laid their eggs. Fishermen realized that they swam out to sea, but that was all they knew. In 1846 a German scientist caught some tiny leptocephali in nets at sea. He did not know that they were larval eels. He thought they were a new form of fish.

Fifty years later, in 1896, another scientist netted some larger leptocephalus larvae in the Mediterranean Sea. He kept them in an aquarium and watched them transform into little eels or elvers. This proved that leptocephali were very young eels. No one knew as yet where they hatched in the sea.

A determined Danish scientist spent many years trying to net eel larvae. He netted the largest elvers close to the shores of Europe and America. He reasoned that these were the farthest from the hatching area. The smaller the larvae, the closer they were to their birthplace.

This man found that the smallest leptocephali of all came from the Sargasso Sea, some 600 miles southeast of Bermuda. They were just a quarter of an inch long and newly hatched. He had finally discovered where eels laid their eggs.

6. Insect Migrations

A few insects are well known for the long journeys they make. In some areas dragonflies migrate in huge swarms. Certain butterflies migrate too. Ships at sea have reported passing through great clouds of them. The best-known butterfly migrant in North America is the big orange and black monarch.

Monarch Butterflies

Monarch butterflies are common insects throughout the United States and southern Canada during the warm months. Two or three generations of them appear each summer. They lay tiny green eggs, and the tiger-striped caterpillars that hatch from them feed on milkweed leaves. When fall comes, the adult butterflies from the last summer generation start to fly south. They often fly in loose flocks that roost together in trees at night.

In the far West the monarch butterflies head for several different wintering areas in California. They

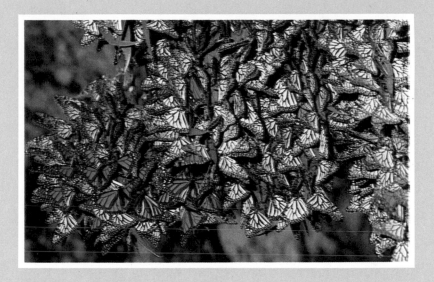

Monarch butterflies gather in huge clusters
on trees at wintering areas.

In summer, monarch
butterflies breed
throughout the
United States and
southern Canada.
They winter in
California and
Mexico.

Wintering Areas

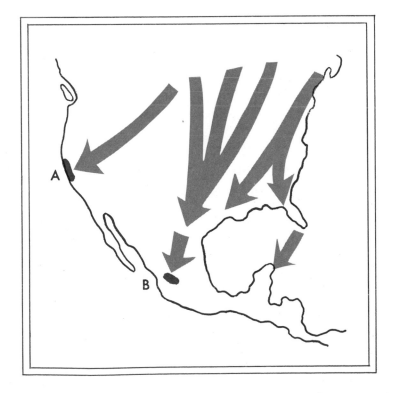

gather in huge clusters on certain trees. When the weather is cold, the butterflies seldom fly or move about; they are semi-dormant. The best-known butterfly town in California is probably Pacific Grove, some 60 miles south of San Francisco. Monarchs gather here in uncounted thousands. Pacific Grove is proud of its title, "Butterfly Town, U.S.A.," and has passed laws to protect its beautiful winter visitors.

In central and eastern North America, monarch butterflies migrate southward to the states bordering the Gulf of Mexico. Most of them continue their long journey until they reach remote forested valleys high in the Sierra Madre mountains of central Mexico. Here they gather by the millions in several winter colonies. Each colony is only a few acres in size. The butterflies spend the winter in these humid and sheltered mountain forests. Sometimes they cluster so thickly on the trees that large branches break under their weight.

The location of the monarch's wintering area in Mexico was unknown to science until 1974, when associates of Dr. Fred A. Urquhart, a Canadian zoologist, discovered one of the principal colonies. Dr. Urquhart has been studying the travels of the monarch butterfly since 1952. He and his associates have fastened tiny paper tags to nearly a quarter of a million butterflies in the effort to trace their journeys. One monarch tagged near Toronto was picked up several months later in a little Mexican town more than 2,000 miles away.

When springtime comes, the butterflies that wintered in Mexico begin the long flight northward. Along the way females mate and lay their eggs. Soon the first of several new summer generations appear.

Swarms of Locusts

The migratory locust of Africa and the Near East is another famous insect traveler. These grasshoppers sometimes gather in migratory swarms that number hundreds of millions, or billions, of insects. Awesome clouds of adult locusts darken the skies as they fly from one area to another. Wherever they descend, they eat every bit of green grass, grain, or other plant life in their path.

Studies show that these destructive migratory locusts are a special variety of the common locust that lives in these regions. Under ordinary conditions the relatively harmless, gray-green insect

Descending upon an area, swarms of migratory locusts
strip the leaves from all the vegetation.

Adult migratory locusts
have fully developed
wings and can fly
quickly from one area
to another.

causes little concern. Solitary and shade-loving, it does not gather in great flocks or migrate from one place to another.

However, under very favorable conditions this relatively harmless locust increases rapidly in numbers. Eventually the insects become very crowded in a given area. The young that hatch from the eggs laid in this crowded area are quite different in appearance and behavior. They are much darker than their parents. As they grow, they gather in huge swarms that hop from place to place, stripping the leaves from all the vegetation in their path. When they become adults, they fly on fully developed wings. Clouds of locusts swarm through the skies, traveling from one area to another. They usually go to areas where there has been recent rainfall. There they can find more food. Some swarms travel thousands of miles.

A World Warning Center has been established to follow the movements of the locust hordes and to develop new ways to fight them. Radar helps to locate the locusts and trace their route, and planes are used to spray them with insecticides.

7. Nomads, Stay-at-Homes, and Emigrants

Army ants of South America do not make long journeys as migratory locusts and monarch butterflies do, nor do they stay in a fixed home. Instead, they travel from one place to another in a constant search for food. They are wanderers, or nomads.

The most important member of the army ant colony is the queen. Only she can lay the eggs that will develop into new colony members.

Army ant colonies also include soldier ants that defend the others, forager ants that hunt for food, and nurse ants that carry and look after the ant eggs and the wormlike larvae.

Marching Army of Ants

Each night the colony of army ants, sometimes hundreds of thousands of insects, march in roving columns from one area to another. Along the way they attack and eat insects, lizards, and other small animals which cannot escape from them. Larger injured or trapped animals are sometimes overrun and

Army ants form a chain between leaves. Large ants with big jaws are soldiers; smaller ants are nurses and foragers.

killed. During the day the ant army stops to rest and eat some more.

After marching for about 17 days, the army camps in one spot for about three weeks. The queen and her helpers settle into a hollow log or other shelter. There the queen lays many thousands of eggs to replace those members of the colony that have died. At this time the legless larvae that the nurse ants carried during the travels become full-grown larvae. They spin cocoons and change into a resting stage called pupae. Before the three-week camping period ends, adult workers emerge from the pupae. Soon the army of ants begins its nightly marches once again.

Mountain lion (left) and wolf (right) do not migrate, but both have large hunting territories.

Home Ranges and Hunting Territories

Many animals never migrate, for they have no need to travel. They find in one area all the food and shelter they need. They also breed and raise their young there.

Mice, shrews, and rabbits usually have home ranges that are small in size, sometimes less than an acre. Large hunting animals, such as wolves, bears, and mountain lions, have home ranges that are many miles long and wide. These big meat-eaters travel through their territories as they hunt for prey. They may make regular circuits of the area as they travel. Sometimes they take several weeks or more to cover a large hunting range.

Some of the animals that do not migrate sleep throughout the winter when food may be scarce. The woodchuck, or groundhog, is very fat when cold weather approaches. It retreats to an underground burrow within its territory and falls into a deep winter sleep called hibernation. It awakens only when warm weather has returned and there is green food for it to eat once again. Chipmunks store food in their underground nests and spend the winter there. They sleep most of the time. Black bears also sleep through the winter in sheltered dens.

Most stay-at-homes are active throughout the year. Pheasant and grouse usually roam the same

White-footed mice remain in the same area the year round. In winter they may move to sheltered homes within their territory.

areas both summer and winter. So do raccoons and foxes. Field mice, rabbits, and squirrels, animals that foxes hunt, are active year round. In winter the mice burrow under the snow to find seeds and roots to eat. Rabbits fill up on buds and bark and twigs. Squirrels build snug nests and store food for the long cold winter.

Mass Exodus of Lemmings

When weather conditions are right and food is plentiful, a particular animal may rapidly increase in number. For example, mice or squirrels may have more frequent litters than usual and more young in each litter. As their numbers increase, the animals become restless. Where there are too many of them in an area, there will not be enough food for all of them. Then a mass exodus takes place. Large numbers of them move away to other regions.

Mass movements of this sort are called emigrations. Lemmings, little mouselike rodents that live in far northern areas of Europe, Asia, and America, are well known for such emigrations. Many of them are eaten by foxes, hawks, owls, and other meat-eating animals while they are on the move. Disease caused by overcrowding or lack of food kills many

When lemmings become too numerous in a particular area,
many of them move out in a mass emigration.

others. By the next year the number of lemmings in
the original area may be small.

This rise and fall in the lemming population may
occur every four or five years. Snowy owls depend
upon lemmings for much of their food supply. When
the lemming population is small, these ghostly
feathered hunters of the Arctic regions may travel
as far south as the northern United States in search
of food.

8. How We Trace Animal Journeys

People have known for thousands of years that birds disappear from their summer homes every fall and do not reappear until the next spring. But they have not known where they go.

The ancient Greeks believed that swallows and many other birds hibernated during the cold months in the mud of marshes. In 1703 an imaginative Englishman wrote a paper claiming that birds flew to the moon for the winters.

Of course, these beliefs were not true. The real facts about the migrations of birds and other animals were uncovered only when scientists began to observe and study their movements.

Today trained observers watch birds in migration and make notes of what they see. They count waterfowl when they arrive at resting places along their flyways. They record shore birds as they pass particular points along the coast. They wait on mountain tops to watch hawks and eagles as they soar overhead.

Using high-powered telescopes, they observe and count night-flying birds as they fly across the face of the moon. They use huge metal plates called parabolic reflectors to pick up and record bird calls. Sometimes they use radar to follow flock movements.

Two students of bird life use a parabolic reflector to record bird calls in a marshy area.

Light planes and helicopters are used to follow the flights of such large birds as pelicans and cranes and the journeys of caribou, antelope, and other large animals. Both planes and ships are used to follow whale migrations. Salmon and other migrating fish are counted as they swim through fish ladders around dams.

Banding Birds

Scientists learn a great deal about animal movements by marking individual animals for identification. Nearly 200 years ago, John James Audubon fastened bands of silver wire around the legs of five young phoebes in a nest near his father's home in Pennsylvania. The phoebes disappeared for the winter, but two of them returned the next spring, much to Audubon's delight. His simple experiment demonstrated that phoebes could find their way back to the place where they had hatched.

Today people band birds all over the world to determine where and how they migrate, how long they live, and other information about them. The U.S. Fish and Wildlife Service oversees bird banding in the United States and keeps the records. The Bird Banding Laboratory in Maryland supplies offi-

A bird bander holds a woodcock gently
while he fastens a metal identifying band about its leg.

cial bird banders with fourteen different sizes of
metal bands. The smallest are designed for hummingbirds and the largest for eagles and other big
birds. Each band has a serial number on it and the
words: "Write F & WL Serv. Wash. D.C. U.S.A."

If a banded bird is captured or a dead or injured
bird wearing a band is picked up, the Service hopes
that the band or serial number will be returned with
information about where and when the bird was
recovered. About 60,000 such reports are received
each year. By studying the information they receive,
scientists learn where different bird species migrate,

how long they live, and many other interesting facts about them.

Records for more than thirty million banded birds are kept at the Maryland laboratory. And every year an additional million or more banding records are added to that total by the more than two thousand official bird banders throughout the United States.

Banders have many ways to capture the birds they band. At wildlife refuges workers bait areas with grain to attract flocks of ducks or geese. Then they fire a charge which propels a "cannon" net over the birds. Many waterfowl are caught and banded after the nesting season. They have molted their flight feathers at this time and cannot fly.

Other birds are banded as nestlings. One enthusiastic bander, Charles L. Broley, was known as the "eagle man." He climbed tall trees to reach the lofty nests of bald eagles in order to band the eaglets. During a long career he banded more than 1,200 of them.

Bats are banded in much the same way as birds except that the bands are clamped around their forearms. Bat banders enter caves and other places where bats roost and catch them in nets.

Tags, Ribbons, and Bright Colors

Instead of bands many animals are marked with identifying tags or collars. Sometimes even ribbons are used. In 1653, Isaak Walton, the English writer, described how ribbons were tied around the tails of little salmon in an effort to find out where they went in their journeys. Today the fish are usually captured in nets or fish traps and marked with metal tags pinned to a fin or to the fat on their backs.

Big sea turtles are often marked with a metal tag

Newly emerged monarch butterfly is marked with a small paper tag before its release.

Numbers are also used to trace animal migrations. **A polar bear,** drugged by a tranquilizing dart shot from a helicopter, gets an identifying number on its rump.

clipped to the rear edge of one of the front flippers. Young whales are "shot" from shipboard or helicopter with a dart or tube, some ten inches long and made of stainless steel. The tube buries itself deep in the blubber of the whale's back. If the whale is killed at some later time and its blubber boiled down for oil, the tube will be found. It has a serial number printed on it and an address: "Reward for returning to Admiralty, London."

Monarch butterflies are marked with a tiny tag

made of adhesive paper. Fastened to the leading edge of a front wing, it bears a number and instructions: "Send to Museum, Toronto, Canada."

Young pelicans are sometimes marked with colored streamers so that their local movements and travels may be traced. A bird's plumage may be dyed a bright color for the same purpose. Many large-hoofed animals, such as deer or elk, are captured and fitted with bright-colored plastic collars that can be seen and identified at a distance. One fearless investigator in Alaska marked big brown bears for sight identification by shooting them with a bow and arrow. The tip of each arrow had a soft sponge filled with harmless paint or dye.

Radio Transmitters and Satellites

Today the movements of many animals are also traced by fitting them with radio transmitters that send out signals on a particular frequency. These signals can be picked up by distant receivers. The animals' locations can be pinpointed in this way.

For birds, a tiny transmitter may be fastened to a leg or a tail feather. Eaglets usually are fitted with transmitters before they leave the nest. Young whooping cranes get them before they learn to fly.

Gigi, a young, nineteen-foot gray whale, had a transmitter implanted in the fat of her back. Her movements in northward migration were followed for seven weeks.

At Chitawan National Park in Nepal, tigers are put to sleep by shooting them with a dart containing a tranquilizing drug. While the tiger is unconscious, it is fitted with a light plastic collar which contains a radio transmitter. Then the tiger's movements can be followed as it travels through its hunting territory. In Sichwan Province, China, the zoologist, George B. Schaller, has recently followed the travels of several giant pandas in the same way.

On Arctic ice fields polar bears have been followed by helicopter, shot with a drugged dart, and then fitted with a transmitting collar. The signals from these bear collars are then picked up by a weather satellite hurtling through space more than 600 miles above the earth. The satellite relays the information received about the bears' movements back to a ground station.

For more than eight months, a weather satellite also traced the travels through the ocean of an adult loggerhead turtle equipped with a transmitter. The movements of elephants and swarms of migratory locusts in Africa have also been followed by satellite.

Every year scientists devise new ways of following animals in their travels. Every year they introduce new research programs for studying animal migrations and for discovering how animals are able to return home to a particular location year after year.

We are learning more and more about the marvels of migration all the time, but many of the facts about it are still unknown. Part of the story of migration will probably always remain a mystery.

Index